RUSSIAN PROVERBS

Chris Skillen

Illustrations by VLADIMIR LUBAROV
In Association with TEXT Publishers, Moscow

Chronicle Books

First published in 1994 by
The Appletree Press Ltd,
19–21 Alfred Street, Belfast BT2 8DL
Tel: +44 232 243074 Fax: +44 232 246756
Copyright © 1994 The Appletree Press Ltd.
Printed in the E.C. All rights reserved.

Russian Proverbs

First published in the United States in 1994 by
Chronicle Books, 275 Fifth Street,
San Francisco, CA 94103

ISBN 0-8118-0539-5

9 8 7 6 5 4 3 2 1

Introduction

Proverbs and traditional sayings are a link between the present and the past. Their imagery draws upon ways and lifestyles that have been eroded by industrialization and urban life. Yet they do not lose their potency because what matters is not the precise form of words, but the irony or wisdom captured when the phrase was first coined. Every proverb has at least two levels. There is, first, the literal sense of the words and second, their irony, or wisdom. But this literal meaning is almost never the more important. The power of the proverb lies in the taking of its irony and wisdom from the past and applying it to a contemporary situation, where the logic of the literal is allowed to play on another, apparently different, situation.

The interplay between literal and hidden meanings has been particularly important in Russia. Over the course of this century, Russia's transition to a modern industrial society has been traumatic, not least because it has been accompanied by the ruthless suppression of dissent. In less difficult times, when it was possible to express discontent in private, among close friends, Russia's treasury of proverbs proved suitably oblique and indirect as a vehicle for people's true feelings about their world. And so these proverbs from Russia's distant past have continued to have relevance, not in spite of social change, but because of it.

Не плюй в колодец – пригодится воды напиться.

Do not spit in the well, for later
you might want to drink.

◆

Не в свои сани не садись.

Do not try to drive the sleigh
that isn't yours.

◆

На чужой каравай рот не разевай.

It is best not to open your mouth wide
at the sight of your neighbor's loaf.

◆

Пьяному море по колено.

A drunk man thinks that the
sea is knee-deep.

◆

В тихом омуте черти водятся.

Still waters run deep.

Куй железо, пока горячо.

Strike while the iron is hot.

♦

Один с сошкой, семеро с ложкой.

What seven can do with a spoon,
one can do with a plough.

◆

Рыбак рыбака видит издалека.

No matter how great the distance, one fisherman can spot another.

◆

Лбом стену не прошибёшь

You cannot break through a wall
with only your forehead.

Портной без штанов, сапожник без сапог.

Just as a tailor lacks trousers,
a shoemaker lacks shoes.

Не руби сук, на котором сидишь.

Do not cut the bough you are sitting on.

♦

Пристал как банный лист.

Sticks like a bath leaf.

◆

Решетом воду не носят.

You ou cannot carry water in a sieve.

◆

Простота хуже воровства.

Naivety can do more harm
than thievery.

◆

Старый друг лучше новых двух.

One old friend is better than
two new ones.

◆

Ночная кукушка дневную перекукует.

One cuckoo singing by night makes more
noise than all the ones singing by day.

◆

Нос вытащит – хвост увязит,
Хвостё вытащит – нос увязит.

Pity the man who pulls his nose out
of the muck only to find his tail is stuck,
and rescues his tail, only to find
his nose in the muck.

Что имеем, не храним,
Потерявши, плачем.

What we have, we lose,
when we lose, we weep.

Стыд не дым, глаза не выест.

It is easier to bear shame
than endure smoke in the eyes.

◆

Гора родила мышь.

Sometimes the highest mountain
brings forth the smallest mouse.

Рыба с головы гниёт.

A fish begins to stink from the head.

♦

Соловья баснями не кормят.

Even nightingales can't live on fairy tales.

Хлеб-соль вместе, а табачок врозь.

Bread and salt may be happily shared,
but tobacco is best kept private.

◆

Лес рубят – щепки летят.

You can't chop down a forest
without splinters flying.

♦

В Тулу со своим самоваром не ездят.

There's no point in taking your samovar to Tula.

◆

Хорошо знает кошка, чьё мясо съела.

A cat always knows whose meat it eats.

Русские волка ноги кормят.

Russian wolves live by using their own legs.

◆

Худой мир лучше доброй ссоры.

Better a bad peace than a good row.

◆

Правда хорошо, а счастье лучше.

It is good to know the truth,
but better to be happy.

◆

С волками жить – по-волчьи выть.

Those who live amongst wolves must learn to howl like wolves.

Что у трезвого на уме, то у пьяного на языке.

What is on a sober man's mind is on a drunk man's tongue.

♦

Не красна изба углами, а красна пирогами.

Do not judge a house by its appearance
but by the warmth of the welcome.

Свои собаки грызутся, чужая не приставай.

It is a brave or foolish dog that
joins a fight between friends.

◆

За двумя зайцами погонишься, ни одного не
поймаешь.

Chase two hares and you'll catch neither.

◆

С милым рай и в шалаше.

Where there is love,
even a hut will seem like heaven.

♦

Посади свинью за стол, она и ноги на стол.

Allow a pig to sit at your table,
and it will put its feet on your plate.

♦

Волков боятся – в лес не ходить.

He who fears wolves will never go to the woods.

Люби́шь ката́ться, люби́ и са́ночки вози́ть.

Those who enjoy skiing downhill
had better enjoy climbing uphill.

◆

Были бы кости, а мясо нарастёт.

If the bones remain, the flesh will come again.

◆

Ворон ворону глаз не выклюет.

One raven does not pick
the eyes of another.

◆

Яйца курицу не учат.

The egg should not try to teach the hen.

◆

Не рой другому яму, сам в неё попадёшь.

Do not dig a hole for somebody else,
lest you fall in it yourself.

Каков поп, таков и приход.

Like priest, like flock.

◆

Старого воробья на мякине не проведёшь.

You cannot catch an old bird
by offering it chaff.

◆

Старая любовь не ржавеет.

Old love does not rust.

◆

Чтобы узнать человека, надо с ним пуд соли
съесть.

You never know a man until you've eaten
a whole sack of salt together.

◆

Кошке игрушки, а мышке слёзки.

The cat's playthings are the mouse's tears.

Бодливой корове Бог рог не даёт.

God sends short horns to a cursed cow.

◆

Господь не выдаст, свинья не съест.

If the Good Lord doesn't give,
the pig doesn't eat.

◆

Яблочко от яблоньки недалеко падает.

The apple never falls far
from the apple tree.

Под лежачий камень вода не течёт.

Water does not flow under settled stones.

В чужих руках ломоть велик.

A morsel looks big in someone
else's hands.

♦

За одного битого двух небитых дают.

One man who's been flogged
is worth two who haven't.

Бумага всё терпит.

Paper will accept any writing.

♦

У семи нянек дитя без глаза.

Give a child seven nannies, and
it is sure to be neglected.

Снявши голову, по волосам не плачут.

It is too late to worry about your hair when you are about to lose your head.